# BLOCK and SILK SCREEN Printing

**By G. ÅHLBERG**

**and O. JARNERYD**

STERLING PUBLISHING CO., INC.
New York

# STERLING CRAFT BOOKS

## PHOTO CREDITS

The authors and publisher are grateful to the following organizations for the photographs in this book:
Art Museum, Basel—81 A; ATA—31, 67; Museum of Modern Art, New York—79, 87 A; Northern Company—51, 59, 81 B, 82, 84, 85, 86, 87 B; Northern Museum—45 B, 71, 78; Swedish National Museum—69; Victoria and Albert Museum—63, 65, 70, 72, 73

# CONTENTS

# THE PLEASURES OF BLOCK PRINTING

People with vastly different professions and occupations find it relaxing to make something with their hands. If this manual work is also creative, it produces a very deep sense of satisfaction. Block and silk screen printing is both a creative and satisfying handicraft, which trains the hand to skill and the eye to taste.

Our aim, in writing this book, is to give directions for printing methods which can be carried out by the school child, the professional man, the housewife—the amateur of any age. Many beginners surprise themselves by the ease with which they learn these methods and by the unmistakeably professional appearance of the prints they make. Many a teen-age girl might enjoy making a tie for her boyfriend and a skirt for herself of a matching pattern. Young children will enjoy making their own book markers and Christmas cards. Housewives can be their own interior decorators — they can make beautiful draperies, curtains, and furniture upholstery. Everyone can make truly personalized gifts, such as scarves, handkerchiefs, stationery, note paper and so on.

Because they take up so little room and use such cheap, easily available equipment, block and silk screen printing are hobbies that can be enjoyed at home, at school, at club meetings, meetings of church groups, and so on.

The many illustrations in this book show the great variety of designs which you can achieve within the limits set by the different techniques.

Block and silk screen printing are not techniques suited merely to repetition or imitation. Through them, you can achieve beautiful and original designs, especially when you have developed a high degree of skill. The printing itself is exciting, and you will probably find yourself, as time goes on, devising your own experimental techniques to create fresh, and often striking, effects.

# HOW TO MAKE BLOCK PRINTS ON CLOTH

### What Is a Block Print?

The block print is a stamp print, and it utilizes the same basic principle as stamping: those surfaces of the block which are not to be colored are cut away with a knife so that the other surfaces seem raised. When the block is pressed against a stamp pad, permeated with the coloring agent, and then against the cloth, the result is cloth with a design in color. When you color the design rather than the background, the cloth is said to have a positive pattern. You can also produce a negative pattern by coloring the background and leaving the design in the original color of the cloth. The block used in block printing is usually made of wood. Hobbyists, however, often make the block from linoleum because

it is softer and more easily carved than wood. In this case, the craft is called linoleum printing and the print itself a linoleum print.

For a discussion of the history of block printing; see page 63.

## Planning and Choosing the Design

Designs based on the repetition of one simple form are good for the beginner to start with. This type of design is fairly easy, and it will teach you a great deal about composition; what you learn from it will be of great value in drawing other types of designs, too. To make the pattern pleasing, you must leave meaningful spaces or intervals between the repeated forms. The form which you choose to repeat can be plain or complex, but in either case, endless variation is possible. The addition or removal of a dot or line can change the entire character of a pattern.

It is essential to plan the design so that the individual forms are evenly spaced and close enough together to give the pattern cohesiveness. Sometimes, by leaving the edges of the cloth unprinted, you form an outline or "frame" which enhances the pattern. Draw a number of designs now, before you even begin to print. Later, you can use the best of them for linoleum or silk screen prints on aprons, skirts, scarves, curtains, pillow covers, furniture upholstery and the like.

In choosing a design, consider the eventual use of the cloth you are going to print. If, for example, you are going to make curtains, use a large, clearly visible pattern that can be seen from a distance. Conversely, you may use small pat-

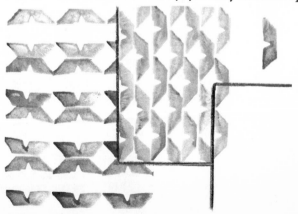

svizeti 1/20

This is a serigraph, a silk screen print on paper designed for solely artistic purposes. It involved the use of 15 colors, some of which were transparent and some opaque. Block and litho stencils were used.

Two different stages in multicolor printing. The left and middle pictures in the top row and the picture at the bottom left show the aqua, magenta and black parts of the design; the picture at the bottom right shows how the three colors fit together to form the final design.

Skirt with silk screen print designed by Inger Sönnergren. Other silk screen prints are shown in the background and inset.

Fanciful, multicolor linoleum prints from Trolltyg,
Bibbi Widmark.

terns for objects, such as pot holders, that will be seen chiefly from near at hand. Don't add adornments at random. Remember that the shape as well as the function must help dictate the design of your cloth. You may want a border around a round cloth, for example, or a round area in the center. On a long, narrow runner you may want a pattern with a clear, lengthwise direction, or lengthwise borders, or, still another possibility, frequent crosswise borders. Cloths which will hang — curtains, aprons or skirts, for example — may require patterns with a clearly upward direction, crosswise patterns which are heaviest at the bottom, or merely a well-defined finishing border.

The same general rules apply both to geometric and figured patterns. Figures, such as people, plants, animals or the like are often too difficult for beginners, though, even those who draw well. Unlike geometric shapes, figures often are suggestive of the things we are used to seeing them with. It is easy to forget that the figures are only a part of the entire pattern and to concentrate on each one as if it were the whole design in itself. If you draw figures, therefore, draw them carefully, of course, but at the same time, keep in mind their relationship to the whole. Another thing to

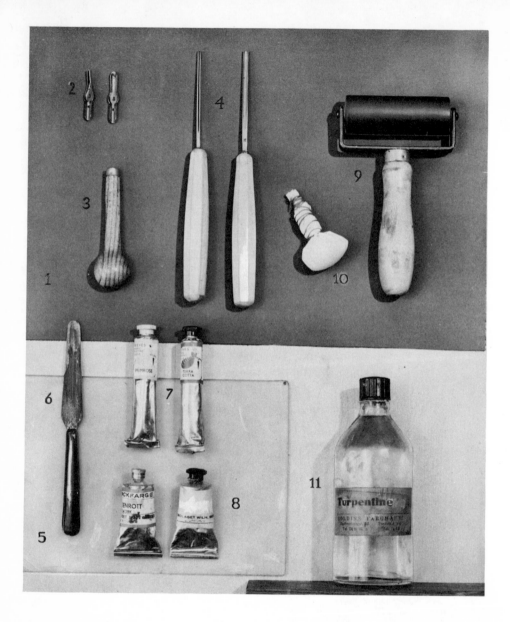

| | | |
|---|---|---|
| 1. SHEET OF LINOLEUM | 5. GLASS PALETTE | 9. ROLLER |
| 2. LINOLEUM CUTTING KNIVES | 6. PALETTE KNIFE | 10. DAUBER |
| 3. HANDLES FOR KNIVES | 7. PRINTING INKS | 11. TURPENTINE |
| 4. WOOD CARVING TOOLS | 8. THINNER | |

keep in mind is the particular printing technique you are going to use. There are no standard rules governing the adaptation of figures to textile design, but if, for example, you are planning a monochrome (one-color) print, remember that you cannot distinguish the parts of the figure from one another by color. You will find enormous leeway for self-expression in cloth printing, even within the limits that each technique imposes or those that you may choose to set for yourself.

## Equipment for Linoleum Printing

You can buy the equipment necessary for linoleum printing in any well-equipped art supply store. The *sheet of linoleum* which you will need for the linoleum block should be plain and at least ⅛ of an inch thick.

Well-sharpened wood carving tools are the best tools you could ask for, but they are quite expensive. If you have access to them, use a small decorating tool and a wider one. Otherwise, use *linoleum cutting knives.* These come in about six different shapes and are numbered according to increasing order of breadth. You will need at least two — No. 1 and No. 5. The knives are inexpensive and you simply replace them when they get dull. Get a *knife handle* as well — the kind that holds the knife the same way that a pen holds a pen point.

A fairly large *glass plate* is desirable to use as a palette, on which to mix and roll colors. Any smooth, flat surface which will not absorb your pigments will do as a substitute. You will also need a *palette knife.* This instrument has a flexible blade, and is indispensable for mixing *oil paints* and

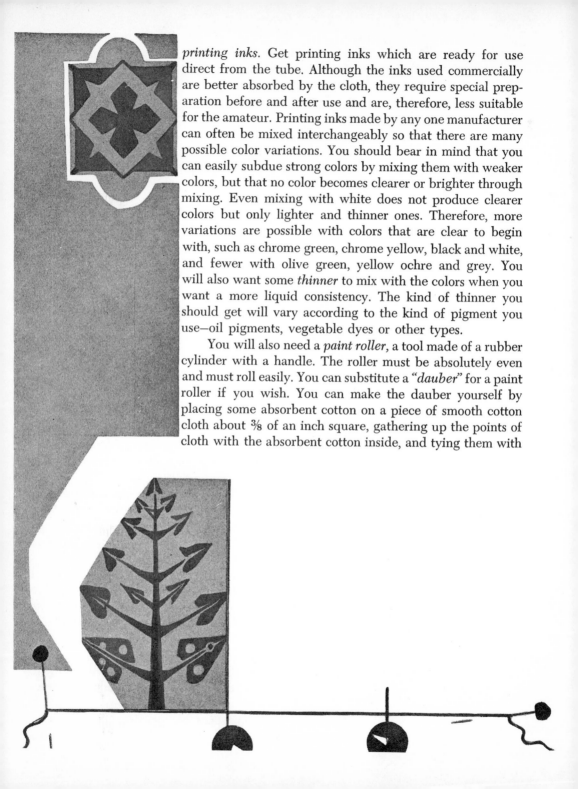

*printing inks.* Get printing inks which are ready for use direct from the tube. Although the inks used commercially are better absorbed by the cloth, they require special preparation before and after use and are, therefore, less suitable for the amateur. Printing inks made by any one manufacturer can often be mixed interchangeably so that there are many possible color variations. You should bear in mind that you can easily subdue strong colors by mixing them with weaker colors, but that no color becomes clearer or brighter through mixing. Even mixing with white does not produce clearer colors but only lighter and thinner ones. Therefore, more variations are possible with colors that are clear to begin with, such as chrome green, chrome yellow, black and white, and fewer with olive green, yellow ochre and grey. You will also want some *thinner* to mix with the colors when you want a more liquid consistency. The kind of thinner you should get will vary according to the kind of pigment you use—oil pigments, vegetable dyes or other types.

You will also need a *paint roller,* a tool made of a rubber cylinder with a handle. The roller must be absolutely even and must roll easily. You can substitute a *"dauber"* for a paint roller if you wish. You can make the dauber yourself by placing some absorbent cotton on a piece of smooth cotton cloth about ⅜ of an inch square, gathering up the points of cloth with the absorbent cotton inside, and tying them with a piece of string or a rubber band. The stuffing should not feel hard but should have some "give." Throw the dauber away after you have used it.

*Turpentine* is good to keep around to remove printing ink and spots and to clean tools and equipment. Other things which are good to have at hand are newspapers, a large sheet of cardboard or an old blanket, pins, thumbtacks, carbon paper, drawing paper and a pen.

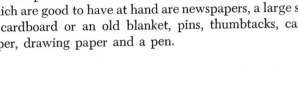

## Choosing Fabrics

The choice of fabrics on which to print is so great that it is easier to warn about the less usable ones. Satin and certain woolen cloths do not take print well; cloths of the hand-woven type do not take a pattern clearly either because their surfaces are so uneven.

Cloths with an even and smooth surface, such as silk, linen, cotton and nylon, are good for cloth printing. Usually people choose a solid-colored cloth to print, but plaids and stripes can also be very modish as a background. You can print on materials of all colors, light as well as dark. Bear in mind, though, that the linoleum print works best if the ink is darker than the background color. Choose cloths of fine quality; with good cloth, you will probably set higher standards for your work, and the results will be worth showing.

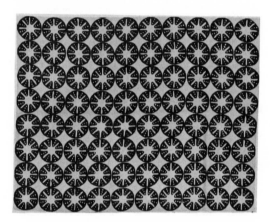

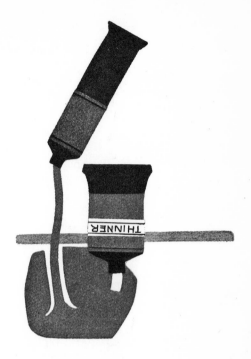

Draw the design carefully on paper.

The next step is to lay the drawing with the carbon paper under it on the linoleum, flush with the topmost edge of the sheet of linoleum and about ⅜ of an inch from the left edge of it. This margin and the one you will later leave on the right side of the block will serve as hand holds. Now trace the drawing. If you don't have carbon paper, blacken the back of the drawing thoroughly with a soft lead pencil. Lay it on the sheet of linoleum in the same manner and trace the drawing just as if there were a carbon paper under it.

Remove the drawing and carbon paper from the linoleum. Carve the outlines of the design with the linoleum knife (No. 1) or a narrow wood-carving tool. Carve lightly enough so that you don't rip the linoleum; if you do, the lines will be ragged. Keep your fingers out of the path of the knife which can slip very easily.

Take the linoleum knife (No. 5) or a broader carving

tool and cut away from those areas which will remain *un-colored* so that the other areas seem raised. Cut some linoleum away from the hand holds, too. See to it that there are no high ridges remaining in the cut-away areas, for the lower and more even the background is, the less risk you run of unintentional spots of color on the cloth. Always remember to cut away from yourself.

Cut the block and hand holds out of the sheet of linoleum with a scissors. Do this very carefully, as the linoleum is very fragile now; so much of it has been cut away that the pattern is visible on the reverse side. Occasionally it might be useful to cut the block in a different shape to suit a special purpose. If, for example, the pattern is to follow certain exact

lines in the cloth itself — perhaps diagonal — cut two diagonal edges, which will then guide you in following these lines in the cloth. Pencil marks or lines on the back of the linoleum block can easily serve the same purpose. Another effective way of constructing guide lines is to place the cloth on a hard surface and stretch strings across it, parallel to the lines you wish to follow. Secure the strings with thumbtacks an inch or so beyond the cloth.

Squeeze out some printing ink on the palette. It is exciting to discover the colors you can make by mixing two or more colors. Mix a small amount with your fingertip and then try the result on white paper or a swatch of the cloth you intend to print. See how the color changes on different backgrounds. When you have decided on a certain color, mix the amount you will need. It might be wise to make more than you need in case you have underestimated. Work the colors together with a palette knife. If the mixed colors feel thick and tough in consistency, use a little thinner. Otherwise the design will be unnecessarily stiff. Don't thin the color too much, though, because then the thinner will spread out in the cloth like grease spots around the design. Notice on the illustration on page 23 the approximate proportions of thinner to ink. You will soon learn just when the color changes consistency and becomes sufficiently pliable. In using these printing inks from the tube, a little stiffness in the finished print is unavoidable but it will disappear when the cloth is laundered.

Scrape the color together into a corner of the palette. Spread out a bit of the color with the palette knife to form a surface about $\frac{1}{16}$ of an inch thick. Roll the paint roller back and forth on the inked surface, until every speck of it is covered with an even layer of color. Then roll it on the linoleum block until all the raised surfaces are colored. If any color sticks to the cutout areas, cut them away more. Otherwise, the block is ready for a trial impression.

You can substitute a dauber for a roller, as you know, although the roller is better for spreading color evenly over large areas. Hold the dauber from the top, dipping the stuffed part a few times into the ink on the palette. Then rub it straight up and down the linoleum block with rapid strokes until the entire design is covered with an even thin film of color.

Place some paper or a cloth (not the cloth you are going to print — first you must make a trial print) on a soft layer of padding. An old blanket, protected with a sheet of rubber, plastic or oilcloth is best, but newspapers piled one on the other or cardboard will do. The main thing is that the padding should lie smooth and absorb whatever color may seep through the paper or cloth. Lift the linoleum block by the hand holds, place it *face down* against the paper or cloth, and press it with your hands, with a cold iron, or by standing on it. If you can avoid sliding, standing is most effective, especially for printing large cloths. Lift up the linoleum block, and there lies the first proof of the print. You can still revise the design if you are not pleased with it, but first wash the color off the block with turpentine.

If you liked the result of your trial impression, you are now ready to print on your good cloth. Fasten it to the layer of padding with thumbtacks or pins, and mark (with chalk) the places on the cloth where you want the design to appear. If the pattern is to be printed in straight lines, construct some guide lines, as described on page 25. Now repeat the same procedure as in the trial impression.

Apply new color to the linoleum block between each printing.

When you have finished the work, clean all your work tools thoroughly with turpentine, including the block if you want to use it again.

If unintended ink spots appeared on the cloth, you can try to remove them by rubbing turpentine on and then carbon tetrachloride. This method may not be successful, though, as the spots usually just get lighter and larger without disappearing altogether.

Hang the printed cloth up to dry for four or five days or longer. Once it is completely dry, the colors will not bleed in the wash. Boiling can have the effect of lightening the colors or of changing them completely.

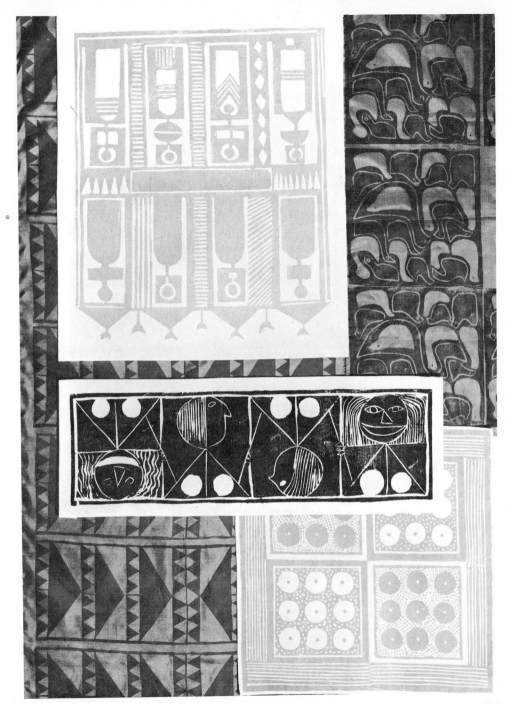

## Using More Than One Color

It is no more difficult to print cloth in many colors than in one color. If the areas to be colored differently are so far apart on the block that you can color them with a dauber without their touching or running together, then you can print all the colors at once. Usually, however, people cut a separate block for each color. The general procedure is the same — the drawing, tracing, carving and so forth. The difference is that, in planning the design, you break it down into its component parts by color. You carve all the parts which are to be of the same color on one block, so that you have as many blocks as colors. In principle, multicolored prints are not more difficult to execute. You must, however, work with extreme precision, carving the different blocks to exactly the same scale. Otherwise they won't fit together properly when you print them. Be sure to carve the blocks deeply enough to make the design visible on the reverse side. This will help guide you in matching the parts together when you print. Designs in which the smaller shapes copy the larger ones, as in concentric circles, are fairly easy to fit together. It is better, when you print, to print the larger shapes first and fit the smaller ones in later. You may also find it helpful to use stretched strings as guide lines.

(Opposite) Early Italian block print on linen. The lettered borders are part of the design.

## How to Make Potato Prints

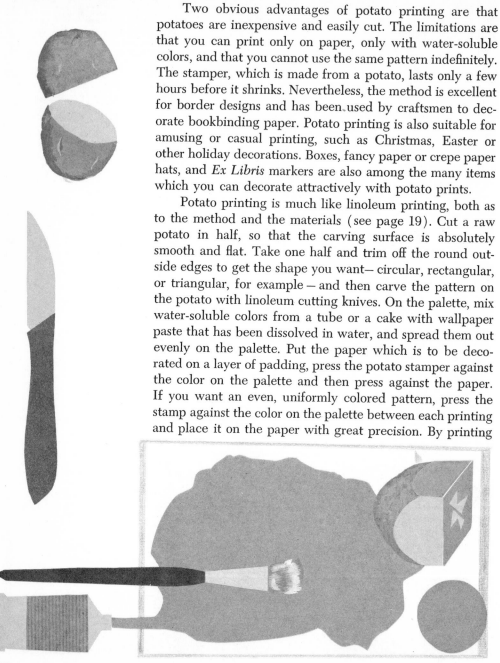

Two obvious advantages of potato printing are that potatoes are inexpensive and easily cut. The limitations are that you can print only on paper, only with water-soluble colors, and that you cannot use the same pattern indefinitely. The stamper, which is made from a potato, lasts only a few hours before it shrinks. Nevertheless, the method is excellent for border designs and has been used by craftsmen to decorate bookbinding paper. Potato printing is also suitable for amusing or casual printing, such as Christmas, Easter or other holiday decorations. Boxes, fancy paper or crepe paper hats, and *Ex Libris* markers are also among the many items which you can decorate attractively with potato prints.

Potato printing is much like linoleum printing, both as to the method and the materials (see page 19). Cut a raw potato in half, so that the carving surface is absolutely smooth and flat. Take one half and trim off the round outside edges to get the shape you want— circular, rectangular, or triangular, for example — and then carve the pattern on the potato with linoleum cutting knives. On the palette, mix water-soluble colors from a tube or a cake with wallpaper paste that has been dissolved in water, and spread them out evenly on the palette. Put the paper which is to be decorated on a layer of padding, press the potato stamper against the color on the palette and then press against the paper. If you want an even, uniformly colored pattern, press the stamp against the color on the palette between each printing and place it on the paper with great precision. By printing

several times without renewing the color, you can create an
illusion of transparency, which may be desirable in certain
irregular patterns.

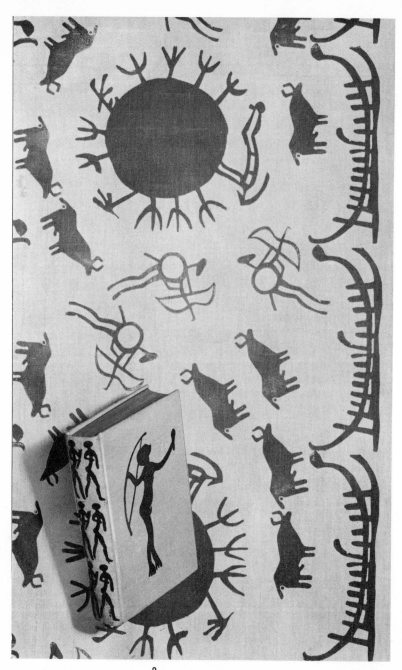

This design by Gudrun Åhlberg, called "African Pastoral," was inspired by paintings by bushmen.

# SILK SCREEN PRINTING

The principle behind the various types of stencil printing, including silk screen printing, is different from that of block printing. Block prints depend on the use of a plate and transfer of the pattern from the plate to the cloth is achieved by means of impression, that is, contact between the plate and cloth. By contrast, however, stencil prints depend on the use of thin, strong materials — the stencil and a porous mesh of silk or cotton — which you lay over the cloth; the transfer of the pattern to the cloth is achieved by the passage of coloring agents through these materials.

The art of producing stencils to decorate cloth goes back very far in time. Archeologists have found stencil prints which are thousands of years old.

Here is a rough idea of the procedure. First you cut out the pattern in metal, leather or other material. Place this stencil over the mesh, which lies in turn over the cloth. Then you spread color in the openings of the stencil. If you move the stencil and repeat the process, you can achieve richly detailed patterns.

Stencil printing is the technique most commonly used today to print textiles. Present-day chemical technology makes it possible to print all kinds of textiles, including synthetic textiles, and there is scarcely a pattern that cannot be reproduced. Even color reproductions of works by famous artists have been portrayed on silk scarves.

Stencil printing is also in widespread use by art instructors, who find it an excellent means of teaching drawing, and by printers, who find it a profitable means of making art reproductions. In its simpler forms, stencil printing is an ideal hobby. You can achieve impressive results from it without too much difficulty.

The instructions that follow may seem complicated, but you will soon see that the entire process is easier than it looks. No one becomes a master immediately but you will find stencil printing interesting and stimulating even in the beginning when you are first learning it.

## Equipment for Stencil Printing

The essential tools for stencil printing are a wooden frame and a squeegee. If you cannot buy them, you can make them easily or have them made by a carpenter. You should also have hair paintbrushes and, for lacquer stencil printing, a special sharp knife and an oilstone to keep it sharp. Keep all your tools clean and in good condition.

*The Frame.* The size of the frame depends on the use to which you will put it. A good size for you to begin with is 15 by 18¾ inches. For this size, if you are making your frame, use four strips of new, planed wood, two of which should measure about 15 by 4 inches, and two 18¾ by 2 inches. Make sure the wood is completely clean and dry; otherwise, the frame may become twisted, and this will result in poor prints. Nail the strips of wood together. Use a bit of glue also to make the frame stronger. Then screw on angle irons at the corners, as the stress is great when the mesh is mounted. Give the frame two coats of shellac so that it will be easier to clean after printings.

*The Mesh.* The mesh, or screen, may consist either of silk or of cotton gauze. Silk is better, but cotton, which is cheaper, is adequate for the beginner. Cotton gauze is more delicate than silk while being stretched, and you cannot stretch it as taut. This is of little consequence to the amateur, however, who rarely uses large frames. Although cotton gauze is good for textile prints, it is a bit coarse for printing on paper.

Silk comes in different degrees of fineness. The higher the number, the more finely meshed is the silk. People usually use a coarse weave for plainer prints and a finer one for designs with many small details. For stencil printing on cloth, No. 6 is suitable, but for printing on paper, you need No. 12 or No. 14.

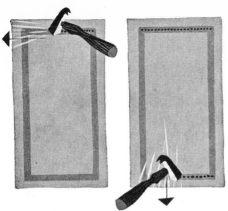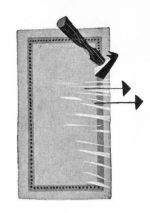

It is even possible to use nylon or metallic mesh, but these materials are expensive and difficult to handle. Avoid the metallic mesh for the time being; it lacks elasticity and is extremely delicate. Despite the difficulties they present, however, both these materials produce excellent prints once you become skilled enough to use them.

You can use the same mesh for many printings because it is washable.

*Stretching the Mesh on the Frame.* First, cut a piece of cloth large enough to extend 1⅞ inches beyond the frame on each side. The excess will provide hand holds. Fasten the corners of the cloth to the frame with short nails or tacks. It is wise to paste the corners down before nailing them. Then stretch one short side tightly and tack down the cloth on the frame. The tacks should be about ¾ of an inch apart. Then stretch and fasten the other short side in the same way. Now repeat the same process with the long sides. You needn't worry about tearing silk, but be very careful of tears if you are using cotton gauze.

After you have stretched and fastened the cloth, wash it with warm water containing a little soda or detergent. This will make the mesh absorb and transmit the pigments more easily.

Lastly, paste a strip of paper along the outer edges of the frame, covering the rows of tacks. It is best to put a strip of paste around the inner edge too. This makes the entire "box" tight, so that no color can ooze out and ruin the print.

When the edges have dried, apply two coats of shellac to the frame.

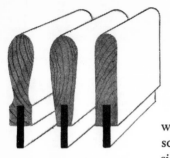

*The Squeegee.* The squeegee consists of a short strip of wood with rubber along one edge. For the frame just described you will need a squeegee of the following dimensions: length—11 inches; height—4½ inches; thickness—¾ of an inch. Preferably the rubber should be synthetic; otherwise, use medium hard natural rubber. The thickness of the rubber should be about 3/16 of an inch and the width about 1¼ inches. Make a groove in the ¾-inch-thick facet of the wood and insert half of the rubber strip into it. The rubber should be straight and even. You can smooth it a bit with sandpaper, a process you should repeat after using the squeegee a while. Otherwise the edge wears down and becomes rounded, producing blurry prints.

*The Printing Table.* An ordinary kitchen table is adequate for making monochrome prints. Spread newspaper over the table to protect it from pigment. If you are using a very large frame or if you are going to print in several colors, attach to the table a surface with hinges, or else equip the table with cleats or nails; this will enable you to hold the frame steady and also to put the frame in exactly the same spot each time.

If you are going to print textiles by the yard, use a long table (page 60). Put a blanket over it and an oilcloth, a sheet of plastic, or a piece of masonite over the blanket. If you use masonite, you will also need a lengthwise strip of wood as a support for the frame. Mark the wood strip with a pencil or a line of tacks for guide marks for the design.

*Racks for Drying.* Some kind of drying arrangement is essential. When you print paper or the like, you can hang it on a string with clothespins or paper clips. Another simple type of drying arrangement consists of a board, on which you stand wicket-shaped wires, as shown at left. You can dry cloth prints by simply hanging them over a line. These prints are fast-drying and once they are dry, you can print again on the same cloth. You must dry printed yard goods overnight before you can roll them up.

*Colors.* For textile printing try to use colors which do not need "fixing" afterwards. Although the resistance of colors to bleeding or fading in the wash is not the most important quality, it is a satisfying and practical one. Before choosing the type of pigment you will use, you must determine which kind of stencil (pp. 44-55) you will work with. Avoid using pigments and stencils which are both soluble in the same material. Oil pigments are the most commonly used by the amateur, and are suitable for all the stencils described in this book. You can also use them for printing both on cloth and on paper. You need merely mix them with plenty of thinner for use on cloth.

The coloring matter should be as thin as possible, since if the colors are too thick the print will be stiff and slow to dry. The color should have about the same consistency as thick cream. You can use turpentine to thin oil pigments and also to remove spots made by oil pigments. When you print on paper, the colors can be thicker, but not thick enough to clog up the stencil.

You should keep jars of oil paint tightly closed. If there is a skin over the top when you open the jar, you can remove it with a stick or a spoon. It is often advisable to strain the pigment through a mesh, after you have mixed the desired color.

Vegetable dyes produce excellent prints on cloth as well as on paper. They dry quickly and are colorfast. There are many attractive colors which, like oil colors, are blendable with each other. Along with the usual colors there is a colorless type, which serves to thin or lighten the colors. Vegetable dyes are translucent as a rule, not opaque. Therefore, you must use only pigments darker than the background. On paper, vegetable dyes produce less clear designs than oil pigments.

A great advantage of vegetable dyes is that you can dissolve them on the screen, thereby eliminating the possibility of its becoming useless due to dried pigment.

With all the types of pigments, it is important to follow the directions on the containers and to use only the recommended solvents. Pigments of different manufacturers may be of different composition and not mixable with one another.

*Fabrics and Paper.* Most fabrics are suitable for stencil printing. Linen, cotton, and rayon produce especially good results. Wool also takes a print well, but has the disadvantage of not being easily washable. Nylon, though printable, takes a great deal of skill to handle, because of its slipperiness; if it slides around during the printing, it can ruin the design. Generally, it is best to start with the cheaper cotton and rayon fabrics. You can print on any kind of paper, although preferably it should be stiff and contain no pulp specks. Charcoal paper is suitable and can be obtained in different colors.

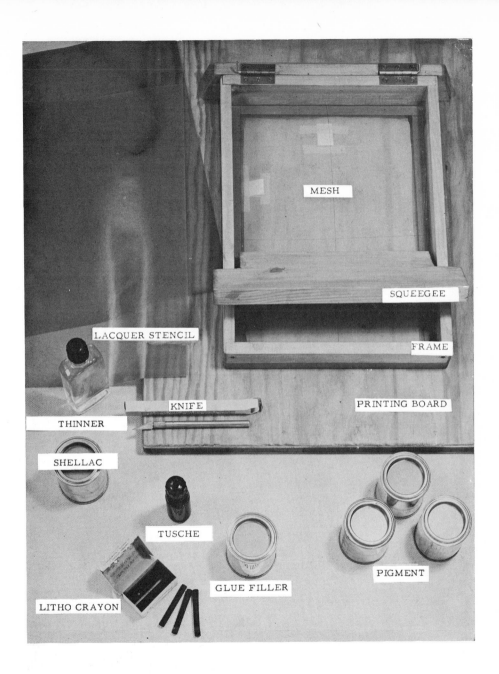

MESH

SQUEEGEE

LACQUER STENCIL

FRAME

PRINTING BOARD

KNIFE

THINNER

SHELLAC

TUSCHE

GLUE FILLER

PIGMENT

LITHO CRAYON

# HOW TO MAKE SILK SCREEN PRINTS

The basic process, common to all kinds of stencil printing, is as follows: using a squeegee, you press pigment onto cloth through the stencil which lies over the mesh, which is stretched on the wooden frame. You cover those areas on the mesh or the overlaying stencil through which you do not want color to pass, with shellac or some other impenetrable material.

You must hold the frame steady, so that it cannot slide. You can hold a small frame with one hand, but a large one must either be held fast with hinges or must lie against a cleat or brace. To use the squeegee properly, hold it parallel to the farther short side of the frame. Pour the pigment onto the screen behind the squeegee, making sure that it does not run between the stencil and the mesh, where it can cause unwanted blobs of color on the print. Pour enough pigment so that you will not suddenly run out of color. With the squeegee, press down and toward yourself. Often, you must do this several times, especially in printing on cloth.

When you finish the work, clean the squeegee thoroughly with a suitable solvent, dry it, and put it aside. Then take a piece of cardboard, roughly the size of the palm of your hand, and scrape up the leftover pigment with it. You can save it for future use or throw it away. Next, scrape as much pigment as possible from the mesh. Then pour a bit of solvent on it and wipe it clean with a cloth or a paintbrush. The weave of the mesh should be completely clean of all color. A certain discoloration of the screen will occur, but this is not important.

## Block Stencil

Block stenciling is the process of forming a stencil by painting directly on the mesh. Obviously, this is the easiest form of stencil. It neither requires nor permits great precision or detail. It is well suited to the creation of simple, forceful designs on textiles. Block stenciling produces patterns with faintly saw-tooth edges rather than sharp ones.

When you use oil pigments to color a block stencil print, apply a heavy coating of shellac or glue to the areas of the mesh which are not to transmit color. Shellac is soluble in thinner, and glue is soluble in water. You can also use glue if you are working with vegetable dyes. The general principle to remember is that the substance you use to make certain parts of the mesh impenetrable must be non-reactive

*(Above)* A single geometric figure, the diamond, is elaborated in various ways in this Scandinavian border print.

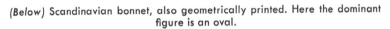

*(Below)* Scandinavian bonnet, also geometrically printed. Here the dominant figure is an oval.

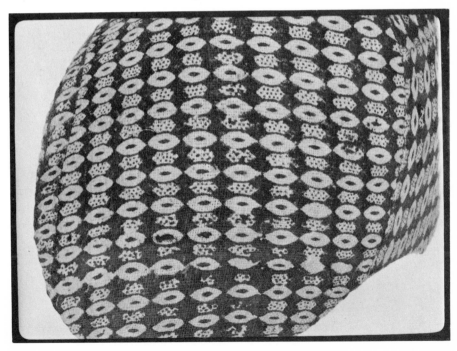

to the kind of color you are using; do not use glue, for example, with water colors. You can use plaster of Paris, which is very effective in preventing color seepage, with all types of pigments. Unfortunately, however, the very insolubility which makes it so effective renders it slightly impractical. You cannot remove it from the mesh, and consequently, the mesh is re-usable only with the same design.

Draw the design on paper. Make the design simple and avoid fine detail. Place the framed mesh over the drawing so that the mesh rests on the drawing (1). Using thin water colors, paint only the outlines of the design on the mesh (2). Leave open those areas of the mesh which are to allow color through, and cover all the other areas with glue or other appropriate filler after the water colors have dried. Use a hair paintbrush and thin the filler to a workable consistency. Place a strip of wood under the frame to raise it a bit and prevent any of the filler from falling and sticking to the table. Check now and then to see that no drops are collecting on the back side of the frame (3). Hold the frame up to the light to see that there are no small "holes" remaining in the filled-in areas. If there are any, wait until the first coat has dried and then fill in the holes. More holes may appear during the drying (4).

Now make a trial proof. Place the framed mesh on some cloth; pour or spread color over the mesh, and with the squeegee, press downward over the whole mesh so that the color is forced through to the cloth (5). If you want to make any changes after seeing the trial proof, wash the color carefully out of the mesh, and let it dry before reworking it.

When the printing is finished, wash the filler and color off the mesh. Place newspapers underneath; these absorb the dissolved dye and facilitate the cleaning up (6). Use the recommended solvents to wash out the colors and the filler.

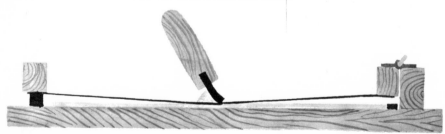

46

# Block Stencil

THE ORIGINAL DRAWING

**1**

OUTLINING THE DESIGN

**2**

SPREADING FILLER ON PARTS OF THE MESH

**3**

HOLDING THE FRAME UP TO THE LIGHT

**4**

PRESSING PIGMENT WITH THE SQUEEGEE

**5**

**6**

WASHING THE MESH

Paper stencil prints are most effective for printing simple, clearly defined but undetailed designs on paper. Because you have to work quickly with this technique, you cannot print large amounts of paper. Usually, people leave the edge of the paper unprinted to form a frame. Since it is difficult to keep the edge clean, however, during the printing, it is better at first to print the whole piece of paper and later mount it in a frame (page 62).

Make this stencil out of waxed paper or oiled paper. Draw your design on ordinary paper and then place it over the wax paper; fasten it to the wax paper with tape or thumbtacks. Cut out the outlines of the design with a sharp knife, and be extremely careful to cut out all the corners thoroughly (1). Now remove the tape or thumbtacks, leaving the stencil loose. Prepare all the color you will need, because this particular stencil process allows no interruption during the printing (2).

Place the frame over the paper so that the mesh rests on it and pour out a little pigment in front of the squeegee. Now bring the squeegee with the color straight across the mesh, pressing fairly hard (4). The object at this point is to get the paper to adhere to the mesh. Turn the frame over and carefully pull off the paper from those places where the color is to come through. The places are marked by the outlines which you cut earlier (5). Paste the outer edges of the sheet of paper to the frame with tape or gummed paper. Now you are ready to make a trial proof (6). The actual printing procedure is the same as in block stencil printing. Put the frame over the paper you are going to print, pour color over the mesh, and press it through with the squeegee. When printing on paper, however, keep the screen about ⅜ of an inch above the paper. Do this by placing a strip of wood under the frame. In this way the contact between the paper and the mesh ceases when you finish pressing the squeegee down. This minimizes the tendency of the paper to stick to the underside of the screen. Remove the paper stencil from the screen immediately after the final printing and wash out the mesh.

# Paper Stencil

**1** CUTTING THE OUTLINES OF THE DESIGN

**2** LOOSENING THE STENCIL

PRESSING THE SQUEEGEE

**3** POURING THE PIGMENT ONTO THE MESH

**4**

**5** PULLING OFF THE PAPER

**6** PASTING THE PAPER TO THE FRAME

## Lacquer Stencil

The lacquer stencil is one of the most useful of the different types of stencil prints. It is commonly used in the commercial printing of placards, advertisements, decorations, streamers and the like. The stencil material consists of transparent paper, thinly coated with lacquer on one side; such paper is available at art supply stores. This stencil is capable of fine detail and the sharpness of the print is unsurpassed. You can use any type of pigment with the lacquer stencil, except vegetable dyes since they dissolve lacquer. This method is also excellent for making prints on ceramic tiles, a hobby which is currently very popular.

It is preferable to use a silk mesh with this stencil.

Draw the design clearly on a piece of paper. Cut a piece of lacquered paper about ¾ of an inch larger than the

(Courtesy of Illini Ceramics)
**Ceramic tile attractively decorated with multicolor lacquer stencil print.**

"Garden of Eden," a surrealistic silk screen print by the Swedish designer Stig Lindberg.    **51**

drawing and fasten it over the drawing with tape or thumbtacks. Take a very sharp knife (have an oilstone on hand to keep the knife sharp enough). Holding the knife like a pencil, cut out the outlines of those parts which are to be colored. The knife should only go through the layer of lacquer and not the paper, although an occasional cut through the paper is not too serious. Poke out and remove the bits of lacquer from those areas which are to allow the color through. The lacquer separates easily from the paper (1).

Place the stencil (still attached to the original drawing) on a sheet of paper, somewhat smaller than the inner dimensions of the frame. Lay the frame on the stencil and press the mesh down against it.

Take two clean, soft cotton cloths, one of which should be dampened with a special liquid (purchasable where you get your stencils) for fastening the stencil to the mesh. Hold one cloth in each hand. Rub the dampened cloth hard on the mesh over the lacquer stencil, making the stencil darken and adhere to the mesh. Don't try to make the whole stencil adhere in one operation. Rather, work successively on small areas. Dry each area immediately with the dry cloth held in your other hand (3).

Let the whole stencil dry for about five to ten minutes. Loosen the paper in one corner and carefully pull the whole layer of it off. You can dissolve isolated bubbles of lacquer which have not stuck to the mesh with a bit of extra dampening (4).

Seal the mesh around the stencil with filler, spreading it with a piece of stiff cardboard (5). Using the same printing procedure as in block stenciling, make a trial proof and then do the final printing. Remove every bit of color from the mesh when you interrupt or finish your printing (6). Use the solvent recommended for the coloring agent you have used. You can wash away the lacquer with thinner.

# Lacquer Stencil

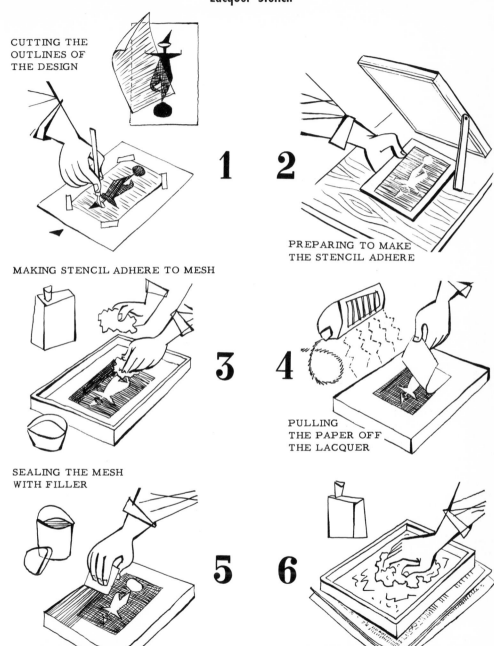

CUTTING THE
OUTLINES OF
THE DESIGN

**1**

**2**

PREPARING TO MAKE
THE STENCIL ADHERE

MAKING STENCIL ADHERE TO MESH

**3**

**4**

PULLING
THE PAPER OFF
THE LACQUER

SEALING THE MESH
WITH FILLER

**5**

**6**

WASHING
THE MESH

# Litho Stencil

Special effects obtained with litho stencil by placing (top) sandpaper and (bottom) linen under drawing.

The litho stencil is most useful for serigraphy (silk screen printing for solely artistic purposes). You can use it to enhance line drawings.

Make a lithographic type of drawing, in which you have stippled areas and small grain effect as well as solid areas. By placing the paper on which you make the lithographic drawing on different backgrounds, you can achieve many varied effects, because you will actually be tracing the surface pattern of the background into the drawing. If, for example, you want a print with a grain resembling that of linen, paste a piece of linen on a sheet of cardboard and put the paper for your drawing on top of that. Other surfaces you might experiment with are sandpaper in different grades and the reverse side of masonite.

Place the drawing under the mesh, which should be made of a transparent silk for this type of printing. Trace the outlines of the design on the mesh with a pencil or thin water colors (1). Place a strip of wood underneath the frame so that it does not lie directly on the table. On the mesh, paint two coats of tusche (an opaque coloring agent similar to lithographic ink) over those parts of the design which are to be colored (2). Hold the mesh up to the light and see that those parts are solid black. This is extremely important, because only the black comes through in the print. In the areas of the design where you want the effect of a chalk engraving, use litho crayon instead of tusche (3). Hold the mesh up to the light again to see that the parts which are to be colored are solid black. When the tusche has dried, spread glue over the whole mesh with a thin, stiff piece of cardboard or a strip of plastic with rounded corners (4). Spread the glue filler from one short side to the other. Then pour out more glue and go back over it the same way, but don't let the coating of glue get too thick. The glue should cover the entire screen up to about 2 inches short of the edges of the frame. Let the glue dry; you can hasten the drying by applying slight warmth. Then pour large quantities of turpentine onto both sides of the screen. After a few minutes, when the tusche and lithograph crayon loosen, wipe the mesh clean (5). You are now ready for the trial impression. The printing procedure itself consists, as you know, of pouring color onto the mesh and pressing it through with the squeegee. After the printing, you can wash the glue filler off the mesh with water.

# Litho Stencil

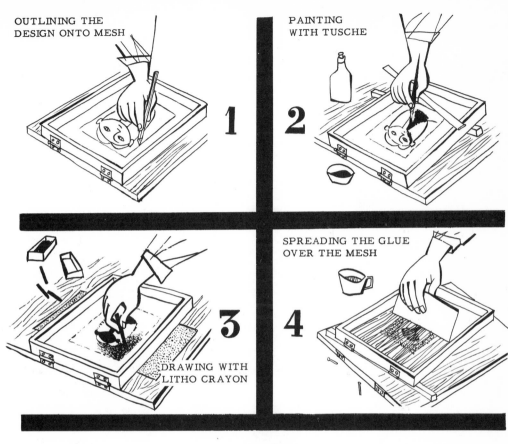

OUTLINING THE DESIGN ONTO MESH

**1**

PAINTING WITH TUSCHE

**2**

**3**

DRAWING WITH LITHO CRAYON

SPREADING THE GLUE OVER THE MESH

**4**

WIPING THE MESH CLEAN

**5**

In addition to the effects shown on page 54, there are other variations with litho stencils. Here ordinary paper, the reverse side of masonite and tusche alone were used.

56

# MULTICOLOR STENCIL PRINTING

Just as multicolor block prints require separate blocks or plates for each color, so multicolor stencil prints require separate screens for each color. While there is no basic difference in method between one-color or multicolor stencil prints, there are slightly different procedures, which facilitate fitting the variously colored parts of the design together. One of these is to mount the cloth on a sheet of cardboard or masonite, on which you have constructed guide marks. The cloth alone is too limp to stay in one place, so that you can print on the same spot with the separate screens, but the cardboard or masonite supplies the necessary firmness. It is also helpful to use two cardboard strips to hold the cloth or paper to the table. These should be long enough to tack one end into the cloth or paper and the other end to the underside of the table. Place the strips at right angles to each other, that is, one on the short side and the other on the long side of the cloth or paper to be printed.

After you have printed one color, put the frame aside. Allow each color to dry somewhat before printing the next. Otherwise, the wet first color will smear the underside of the screen, and this will result in unintended spots on the cloth.

It is often useful to trace the outline of the design on a transparent paper, which you can later use to compare the colors of the actual print with those of the original drawing.

Give thought also to the possibility of overprinting (printing one color on top of another) and to the use of transparent color combinations which are available ready-made. To overprint, you pour out the two colors one behind the other in back of the squeegee. The colors should overlap somewhat. When you move the squeegee across the screen, the colors mix with each other without marked borders.

If your over-all design is multicolored, but the individual whole patterns within it are of one color, then it is better not to print consecutively each space in which a pattern is to appear. Rather, print all the patterns of one color first, leaving space for the patterns of a different color; when all the patterns of the first color have dried, print, in the spaces you left, the patterns of the second color, and so on with as many colors as you are using.

Two silk screen prints with slightly irregular designs based on geometric figures. Both prints are by Viola Grasten.

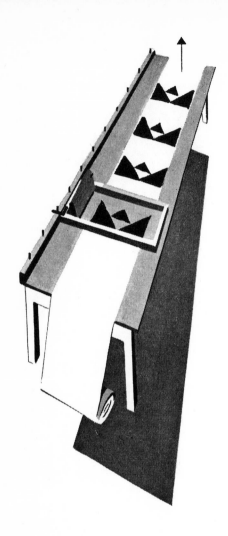

# PRINTING LONG BOLTS OF CLOTH

If you are going to print cloth by the yard, you need a table at least two yards long. Roll the cloth out and fasten it to the table with tape or thumbtacks. Do not stretch it so tight that the fibers get twisted. Put a cleat or guide board along the edge of the table, with guide marks placed at intervals corresponding to the size of the print. You can draw such marks along the guide board or use tacks or nails to indicate the appropriate spots. When you print, walk along the length of the table, moving the frame along by hand. When you have finished the printing, take the cloth off the table and hang it up on a drying rack. Fasten the next bolt if you are printing more than one, and be careful to print the design in the corresponding area of the new bolt.

When you work with multicolor prints on yard goods, take care that the colors do not dry in the frames which you are not using. Placing a piece of cardboard over the frame slows the process of evaporation and helps keep the mesh moist longer.

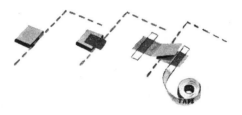

## FRAMING

As a rule, people frame silk screen prints under glass. It is customary to number the supply to indicate how many there are of the same kind. Do not roll up unframed silk screen prints on paper, but, rather, store them flat.

# HISTORY OF BLOCK PRINTING

15th-century block print from a
German workshop.

## First Uses in Europe

Block printing was the first cloth printing method used in Europe. Like most printing methods, the block print came to Europe from the Orient. Although it had long been in use in the East, it did not begin to flourish in Europe until the 1100's. European craftsmen soon found that it took less time to print a design on cloth than to paint it, as they had been accustomed to do. Another advantage was that it enabled the craftsman to reproduce exactly the same pattern many times. Heraldic animals, leaves and branches were the designs in fashion and the print was almost always black on a colored cloth background, often in combination with super-imposed gold or silver.

## Flocking

Silver and gold were applied by a process called *flocking*, which uses a method somewhat similar to the block print. The main difference is that you dip the cutout design in glue rather than in dye and then press it against the cloth. Before the glue dries, you scatter gold or silver dust over the cloth. The dust adheres to the glued parts of the cloth and falls away from the rest of it. Besides gold and silver, you can use the flocking method with various substances ranging from glass dust to finely cut wool.

## Imitations of Fabrics

Block printing replaced not only the painting of cloth, but it also served to produce imitations of other fabrics. Early printed fabrics have been found with patterns so similar to weavings of the same period that the block printer must have copied the design on his wood block. The block printer's models were usually costly Italian brocades, velvets and silk damask. In all probability the printed imitations were coveted by the middle classes who could not afford the magnificent originals.

Even though the printing procedure required a well-planned and careful preparation, especially in the carving of the design block, it became widespread quite rapidly, producing fabrics that were cheap compared with the cloths being copied. It was some time before block printing was again regarded as an independent artistic handicraft, capable of producing fabrics beautiful in their own right and not merely as imitations. In the interim block printers did not always slavishly copy other materials; often they subtly altered or adapted designs in a way that made them particularly suitable for block printing. After several generations' work and experimentation, an independent and masterful printing technique was attained by the 1400's. There are superb materials from that time still in existence.

"Offering to Cupid," an 18th-century engraved print by
Jean-Baptiste Huet. Note the sharp delineations achieved
by engraving.

## The Printing Press

The best and the largest number of workshops were in Germany. There, craftsmen did many experiments with printing, not only on cloth, but also on leather and paper. The most significant result of the experiments was Gutenberg's invention in 1436 or 1437 of the printing press, basically an assemblage of pieces of movable type, operating on the same principle as block printing. Previously books had been made of parchment, the text hand-lettered, and the illustrations painted by the monks in cloisters. As a result books were so expensive that they either remained in the cloisters or were collected only by the very rich. Once the printers took over the monks' role, they produced books in quantity. They replaced parchment with paper and printed illustrations on it which had been cut in wood, exactly as in block printing. These "block prints" on paper are called *woodcuts*.

Early woodcut depicting Adam and Eve in the Garden of Eden.

Elaborate Italian designs. Background is a Venetian design on linen; inset a
Florentine design on silk.

In the 1500's cloth printing was on the decline. It received new impetus, however, in the 1600's, as a result of the introduction into Europe of fabrics from India. After the formation of the East India companies by the great European powers — Portugal, the Netherlands and England — vessels began to ship home multitudes of exotic wares, including flowered chintz from India, the like of which had never been seen before in Europe. It was a multicolored washable and colorfast cotton cloth, which had gone through painting and coloring processes not yet known in Europe. The cloth alone was a surprise for the Western countries, where nothing but silk, wool and linen had ever been woven; furthermore, the elegant flowered patterns and the lasting colors aroused great admiration and the chintzes soon became fashionable both for clothing and home décor. The demand at last became so great that the wool and silk weavers in England, France and Germany feared for their future and appealed to the governments of their countries to end the importing of the popular printed materials. Even though their efforts had a brief success in various places, the ultimate result of the importing was to force the European workshops to produce similar cloths. European craftsmen began first to imitate the coveted designs in block print, but in time they also learned the secrets of the Oriental coloring methods.

The India print designs had black painted outlines. The Indian cloth printers obtained blue by covering the entire cloth with warm wax, except those surfaces which were to be blue. They dipped the cloth in an indigo blue bath, in which the wax protected the background but not the uncovered surfaces from the dye. Then they removed the wax with boiling water. They obtained gold by hand-painting and green by painting gold over indigo blue. They obtained red by waxing those surfaces which were not to be red, by applying various red dyes to the cloth, and finally by soaking it in a dye bath made from the madder plant. This last step was necessary to bring out the red dyes.

An example of the colorful India chintz cloth that became so fashionable in Europe in the 17th century.

## Copperplate Engraving

During the period when it was forbidden to import Oriental cloth into some parts of Europe, domestic cloth printing enterprises began to thrive. Among them was the factory of Christophe Philippe Oberkampf in Jouy-en-Josas, near Versailles, from which comes the 18-century cloth print "Offering to Cupid" (page 65). This is a well-drawn representation of a typical French group; it has a light background with figures and groups casually arranged over the surface of the cloth. If you examine the execution of the design carefully, you will note that it could scarcely have been cut from wood. In order to produce such fine lines, you must cover the wood block, as the craftsman of this cloth did, with a copperplate, on which the design is engraved, or incised. You rub the plate with color and then wipe it off, so that the color remains only in the incised areas. You press the plate firmly against the cloth, a process which then causes the fine-lined design to be reproduced on it. At the time when the illustrated print was made, the technique of copperplate engraving allowed the use of only one color.

## The Industrial Revolution

The Industrial Revolution of the late 1700's transferred the practice of cloth printing from the craftsman's atelier to the factory, where many technical innovations were put into effect. Block and copperplates were placed on cylindrical rollers. Using the principle of rotation, these rollers could print long bolts of cloth quickly and continuously. Newly discovered synthetics replaced the old plant dyes. New possibilities arose, and virtually any pattern or color could be printed. In spite of the technical advances, however, the quality and beauty of the prints declined. In the late 1800's, in protest against the uninspired textile prints coming out of the factories, there arose small workshops like the earlier ateliers of the skilled artisans. The most famous of these workshops was that of William Morris in London. The patterns from his shop, all of which he designed himself, were printed in the traditional block print with the older, more delicate and more substantial plant dyes.

Typical rose design of the 1800's.

Intricate block print by the famous English decorator William Morris.

Many experimental workshops, some of which have a direct connection with industry, still exist in Europe. They often create new types of patterns which are then modified by industry for mass production. Some contemporary hand craftsmen use block printing or linoleum printing. Textiles which bear the label, "hand printed," are usually made by stencil print, which together with photoprint is the most recently developed printing technique.

This multicolor block print on cotton cloth was made in a French workshop, using the chintz coloring techniques that were transmitted to Europe from India.

# OTHER PRINTING AND DYEING METHODS

## Photoprinting

The result of photoprinting is unpredictable but the procedure is easily understandable to the person who does his own photographic developing. The printing process occurs in the darkroom, where the only ray of light comes from behind the negative. You use special preparations which make the cloth sensitive to light, then expose it to the ray of light through the negative, and finally develop and fix the design (make it permanent) in various baths. The method is complicated and difficult; it prints the cloth in only one color, but in different tones or hues, whereas the printing methods described earlier print in only one color tone. In the United States, the most photographically minded country in the world, the photoprint is used to print souvenirs, such as scarves and handkerchiefs. Technically, there is nothing to prevent the production of household fabrics, or materials for clothing with photographic prints of wedding pictures, the summer cottage, the Paris vacation, and so forth. Nevertheless, such cloths are rarely printed, probably because the novelty of photography has worn off, and the trend in modern design is to get away from the photographic illusion.

## Resist Printing

Resist printing is similar to block printing. However, instead of coloring the carved design on the wood block by dipping the block in dye, you dip it in wax, clay, paste, glue or another protective coating and then print it on the cloth. You then put the cloth in a dye bath. Later, when you remove the coating, the protected areas retain the original cloth color. You can treat the cloth and block with various soaking methods and with etching chemicals, which alter the colors. Resist printing flourished for only a short time in Europe because it was not a direct and economical procedure.

## Batik

Batik is a dyeing method of the resist type. You paint or print the cloth with warm melted wax and dip it in dye. When you remove the wax, which is easily broken, the result is a colored design on both sides of the cloth. Where the wax protected the threads, the cloth retains its original color. Batik produces a crackled surface which is its special characteristic. It was originally a bark-dyeing method, used by the natives of Java to design their silk (right). Europeans learned about it through the Netherlands' colonization of Java.

**Batik print designed by Anna-Lisa Feuk.**

# Tie and Dye

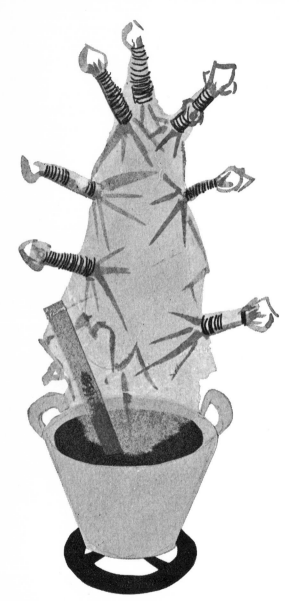

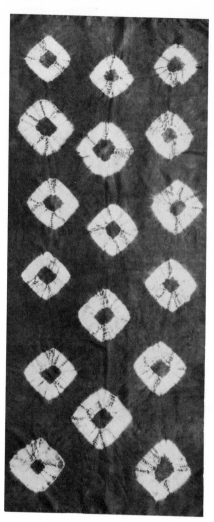

Example of tie and dye on silk; this design is by Mona Nilsson.

## Tie and Dye

The tie and dye method is in some respects a simplified batik. You gather up the cloth here and there and tie it tightly with waxed string or thread. Then you immerse it in the dye bath. When you remove the string you have a dyed cloth with undyed dots, rings or squares. Despite the simplicity of the design, you can obtain many variations by dipping the cloth in different dye baths, moving the knots between baths, and by using colored thread for tying. Resist printing, batik and tie and dye all greatly influenced European handicrafts.

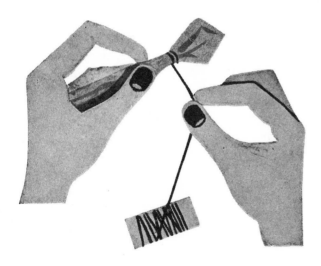

# TYPES OF DESIGN

## Influences on Design

The prevailing fashion and the available technical resources of the times influence the designs in cloth printing, just as they influence the other arts and handicrafts. As flighty fashion changes, the people demand different types of designs. At one moment they want a naturalistic style and at the next abstract. The motifs change. Suddenly a new fad appears, is publicized and becomes popular for a time, until people tire of it and look for something different. The Gothic period has its leaves, the Renaissance its branched-apple pattern, the Rococo period its snails and delightful flowers, the Neo-Classic period its rows of flowers and medallions, and the 1800's its roses (left and pages 71-72).

While many designs of the 20th century grow out of the abstract designs of the late 1800's, they are also closely related to contemporary developments in painting and architecture, which ultimately mold the popular taste. The current tendency in modern design is to use very simple forms, to avoid wholly naturalistic or representational design, and to portray both foreground and background on one plane, with no illusion of perspective. The number and variety of themes is larger than ever, and it is difficult to single out one particular favorite.

## Abstract Design

Abstract designs, such as dots, plaids or stripes, consist of more or less complex geometric shapes. Their popularity is partly due to the evolution of abstract art, as demonstrated around 1907 by the cubist painters Braque and Picasso, who broke up naturalistic shapes into their geometric components (page 87). Such design is mainly non-representational and depends much on color and form *per se;* the most extreme result of this type of painting is the work of Mondrian (right), where clear and clean composition is of great import, as it is to his follower, Astrid Sampe (also right). Cloth prints by Viola Grasten (page 59) have patterns of black, white, and strong, deep colors.

Composition by the Dutch painter Piet Mondrian is superimposed on cloth print inspired by his style. The cloth, called "Modulor," was designed by Astrid Sampe.

## Primitive Design

Primitivism is another 20th-century development which has influenced many textile designers. Primitivists are artists who deliberately use the child's manner of expressing himself in pictures. They also find inspiration in folk art. Page 83 shows a child's drawing based on an old Czechoslovak peasant design. Both the peasant-painter and the child are reluctant to leave much blank space. This unifies their pictures, which is an advantage in textile design. The figures are not arranged in any special order but the horses' long horizontal backs in contrast with the women's large round skirts give the pattern balance and visual interest.

In Sweden the Jobs family has adapted the old folk arts in naturalistically drawn designs, based on story themes from folk songs and paintings from the valleys (pages 84-85).

## Surrealist Design

On page 51 and page 81 there are illustrations of textile prints by Stig Lindberg, who until now has had most success with narrative, representational design. He usually portrays thin, drawn-out figures of a certain ethereal elegance. In his pictorial storytelling he injects amusing little fantasies and strange events, which make his art surrealistic; the subjective, or inner meaning is more important than the outer form. The meaning here derives from the subconscious mind, the soul's secrets and the dream world of disguised symbols. The Surrealists have made a picture-world of the fantastic, in striking contrast with realistic scenes.

*(Right)* "The Burning Giraffe," surrealist painting by Salvador Dali.

*(Below)* Silk screen print, "Pottery," by Stig Lindberg shows surrealist influence.

Two examples of timeless design, based on pure repetition.

*(Left)* "Vallmo," by Helga Foughts.

## Timeless Design

Apart from plaids, stripes and dots, and their many variations, the designs which survive changes of fashion are often those which are constructed by the repetition of a single form or figure. Sometimes contemporary textile designers execute such designs (illustrations at left) along with, or in addition to, their more characteristically 20th-century work.

*(Left)* "Blue Rings," by Kersti Eddes.

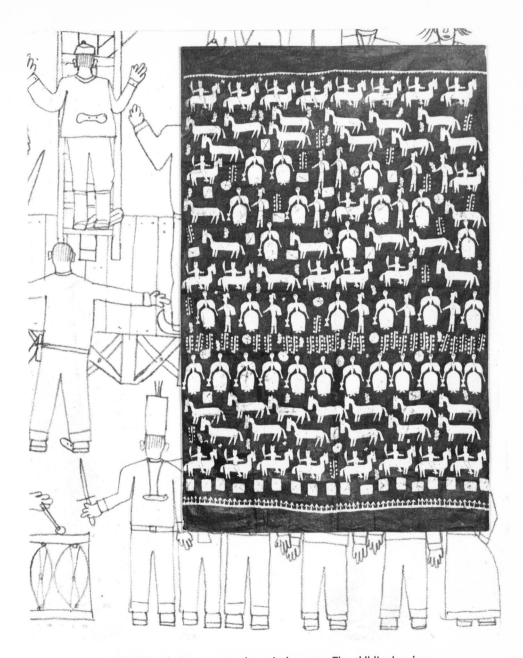

Primitive design goes on through the ages. The child's drawing in the background is based on the old Czechoslovak peasant design shown in the inset.

(Opposite) Primitive designs by the Jobs family. (Inset) Detail from "Banquet Tapestry," by Peer Jobs. (Background) "Swedish Midsummer," by Gocken Jobs.

(Below) Another Jobs design, "1800's," by Lisbeth Jobs.

(Above) Silk screen print made for the Malmö State Theatre, Sweden, by David Helldén.

(Left) Print entitled "Grazia," executed by Stig Lindberg.

(*Above*) "Fernande," by Pablo Picasso.

(*Below*) Detail from "Wedding Picture," by Gocken Jobs.

# INDEX